IT'S YOUR STORY — PASS IT ON

Mary Louise N. Colgin

and

Thea Simons van der Ven

Colgin Publishing

IT'S YOUR STORY—PASS IT ON
Copyright © 1986 by Mary Louise N. Colgin
and Thea Simons van der Ven

All rights reserved. Printed in U.S.A.

Library of Congress Number 86-070785

ISBN 0-9604582-2-0

Colgin Publishing
Box 301
Manlius, NY 13104

Other Colgin publications: *Chords and Starts
for Guitar and Autoharp,* 1980, and *Chants for
Children,* 1982.

We dedicate this book to each of you—known and unknown—who has made a difference in our lives.

Mary Louise N. Colgin

Alec Simon van der V—

All clean and comfortable I sit down to write.

— JOHN KEATS

Biting my truant pen, beating myself for spite, 'Fool,' said my Muse to me, 'look in thy heart and write.'

— SIR PHILIP SIDNEY

I should not talk so much about myself if there were anybody else whom I know as well.

— HENRY D. THOREAU

I never travel without my diary. One should always have something sensational to read on the train.

— OSCAR WILDE

They are children of many men, our words; the blank page, difficult mirror, gives back only what you were.

— GEORGE SEFERIS

All sorrows can be borne if you put them into a story.

— ISAK DINESEN

Getting to Know You.
Who, ME?
Yes, YOU!

Did you ever keep a diary: one of those little books with a lock and key and five lines to record your day? "I went to school today. Mary Jane came to my house. We played." Such entries don't tell much about you. When you write and tell your story—your experiences—you make the usual unusual, the ordinary extraordinary, and you begin to see how very special and unique you are. No one else has the same story as yourself.

Nor can anyone tell us if our story is right or wrong; after all, it is our own and we are the creators.

For most of us, the first and last time we wrote our story was for a seventh-grade homework assignment. Rarely does anyone ask us to tell our story and rarely do we ask others, yet we all have a longing to connect with others in a meaningful way.

Our intention in creating this book, your book, is to help you weave meaning and identity from your memories and experiences.

Stories connect us with each other and with ourselves. Perhaps you have thought: "There's a missing link in my story. I wish I knew more about my father." You can start to make a link for someone you care about by sharing it with a child, a friend, or a relative. Or you may choose to write it just for that very special person: YOU.

This book is for anybody at any age at any time. No questions need to be answered completely at one sitting. It may seem as you start to respond to questions that you can't recall much. Perhaps you will remember a sound. Write about it. Perhaps a smell. Write about it. A touch? Write about it. What you start to write may only be the seed you plant at that moment. This will take time and not be easy, but go back and nourish it from time to time with other thoughts and memories. Watch it grow, blossom, and flower. It may even bear fruit. If you need more space to answer a particular question, use the blank numbered pages in the back of the book.

We hope you will enjoy writing your autobiography, telling your stories, reflecting on the myths and models that have influenced your life. We trust that by telling your stories of joy and pain, fulfillment and disappointment, wonder and fear, hope and despair you will increase your joy, lessen your fear, laugh at what made you cry, share a few tears, and pass on the hope and the love of your journey—the road well traveled.

BON VOYAGE!

Where were you born? Name your mother and father. Where and when were they born? What do you know about your family name?

Do you know how you got your name? How do you feel about it? Did you have a nickname? How did you get it? Do you still use it?

What were your brothers' and sisters' names? Where did you fit in the family picture? What are your early memories of them? If you didn't have brothers or sisters, write about how that was for you.

Father calls me William, sister calls me Will, mother calls me Willie, but the fellers call me Bill.
— EUGENE FIELD

Do you have stories about other relatives who lived in your home with you?

. . . any neighbor stories?

5

Did you live in more than one house? Where: town, country, city, suburbs, hamlet? How old were you when you made each move? How did you feel about moving? What happened once you got there?

I remember, I remember the house where I was born. The little window where the sun came peeping in at morn.
— THOMAS HOOD

Did you ever have a favorite room or place? Did you share it with anyone or did you keep it to yourself? Draw a picture of it or describe it.

Edward the Confessor
Slept under a dresser.
When that began to pall
He slept in the hall.
— E.C. BENTLEY

7

What did your father do? What stories do you remember about him?

"That's another story," replied my father.
— LAURENCE STERNE

What did your mother do? What stories do you remember about her?

.

Who ran to help me when I fell,
And would some pretty story tell
Or kiss the place to make it well?
My mother.
— ANN TAYLOR

9

What do you remember about your grandparents and your great grandparents? Aunts? Uncles? Cousins? Nephews? Nieces?

Who was your favorite relative? Why?

If one of the skeletons came out of the closet, what stories would it tell?

It is in truth a most contagious game: hiding the skeleton shall be its name
— GEORGE MEREDITH

Did your family hit any snags, such as a loss of job, major accident or illness, or sudden additional burden? How was that handled? How did it affect your life?

Tell about your happiest day. If you can think of more than one, write about each one.

14

Tell about your saddest day(s). How did it affect your life?

Did your family have visitors? Who? Where did they come from? How long did they stay? Did you look forward to their visit?

What do you remember about family friends?

Friends depart, and memory takes them to her caverns, pure and deep.
— THOMAS HAYNES BAYLY

What do you remember about family feuds?

Some people can stay longer in an hour than others can in a week.
— WILLIAM DEAN HOWELLS

How did you celebrate birthdays . . .

18

. . . holidays or other special times?

And young and old come forth to play on a sunshine holiday.
— JOHN MILTON

What happened at your house on Sundays?

Did you have family rituals: daily, weekly, monthly (Saturday night bath, whether you needed it or not, or chicken every Sunday, whether you liked it or not)?

How old were you when you had something special like a Teddy Bear or imaginary friend? Tell about it and draw a picture of it.

What did your mother and father tell you about as a child? What stories do you treasure?

What kind of pets did you have? Names? Who took care of them? Did they ever have an adventure? How did you absorb their death or loss?

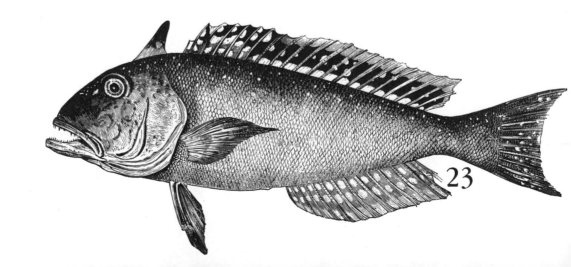

23

Tell about your favorite toys, games, or playtime activity. Who gave them to you? Played them with you? Where? When? Do you still have some?

What do you recall about the first movies, plays, ballets, circus you ever saw? Which ones would you like to see again and with whom? Were there any you wish you had not seen?

Did you like to play outside all year round? What did you do and what kind of equipment was needed? Did you have a special place to play?

How and where did you spend your summer days and evenings?

Who read to you? Sang to you? Told you stories? Tell about those times.

What have been your favorite songs? Stories? Poems? Books?

What was the earliest story you recall. Write it here.

Did you take special lessons for music, art, or sports? What do you remember about them? How do you feel about them now? Do you still have these skills?

Blessed are those that have no talent.
— RALPH WALDO EMERSON

What do you remember about the first day you went to school? Who took you? What did you wear? What equipment did you take? What about other first days?

Who were your favorite teachers and why?

Ah God! Had I but studied
In the days of my foolish youth.

— FRANCOIS VILLON

Who were your least favorite teachers and why?

33

Who teased or played tricks on you? What did you do about it? What would you do about it today?

Who and how did you tease? What were the consequences?

34

Who was your first friend? What did you do together? What happened to that friendship?

What became of the friends I had
With whom I was always so close
And loved me so dearly?
— RUTEBEUF

What did you like to do by yourself?

36

What were some of your secrets?

Did you do naughty things? Were you caught? What happened then?

If you do something wrong, at least enjoy it.
— TALMUD

How old were you when you first asked "Is there a real Santa?" Who answered and how? Does one gift stand out in your memory as the most favorite, sublime thing you ever received and still casts a spell?

> *Man, if you gotta ask, you'll never know.*
> — LOUIS ARMSTRONG

What tasks did you have around the house? How did you like them? When did you do them? Were you paid for them?

Did you have any money to spend when you were a youngster? Who did you get it from and what did you do with it?

What did/do you like to eat? What did/do you hate to eat?

"It's broccoli, dear."
"I say it's spinach, and say the hell with it."
— ELWYN BROOKS WHITE

Describe your favorite outfit. When and where did you wear it? What happened to it? How did it come to you?

Describe your least favorite outfit. When and where did you wear it? What became of it? How did it come to you?

It would have made a cat laugh.
— JAMES ROBINSON PLANCHE

43

What do you like to remember about your first sweetheart(s-s)?

It shall be inventoried, and every particle and utensil labeled to my will: as, item, two lips, indifferent red; item, two gray eyes, with lids to them; item, one neck, one chin, and so forth.
— WILLIAM SHAKESPEARE

44

Were you ever afraid of the dark? What nightmares can you remember? Was there someone to help you with your fears? What did s/he do?

Don't tell me what you dream'd last night,
for I've been reading Freud.
— FRANKLIN ADAMS

45

How did you first learn about the facts of life? What were your first "facts"? When did you become aware that you were a boy or a girl? How did you feel about that?

I wonder what Adam and Eve think of it by this time.
— MARIANNE MOORE

I love the idea of there being two sexes, don't you?
— JAMES THURBER

Who were the people who helped you develop your understanding of yourself? Did you have a mentor?

Do you have a rite-of-passage story: fairy tale, folk tale, your own story?

Were you ever caught in a storm? Was it exciting, scary, or both for you? Tell the story.

49

What made you laugh? What made you sad? What made you angry?

Wit is the only wall between us and the dark.
MARK VAN DOREN

To laugh is proper to man.
— FRANCOIS RABELAIS

50

What was your biggest disappointment when you were young? Now?

It always was the biggest fish I caught that got away.
EUGENE FIELD

What was so great about the best vacation(s) you ever had?

Give the gory details of the worst vacation you ever had?

*Beyond the East the sunrise, beyond the West the sea. And
East and West the wander-thirst that will not let me be.*
— GERALD GOULD

Who were and are your heroines and heroes?

Neither the lords nor the shogun can be depended upon to save
the country, and so our only hope lies in grass-roots heroes.
— YOSHIDA SHOIN

Every hero becomes a bore at last.
— RALPH W. EMERSON

Who was a wise person in your life? You may have had more than one. How did they affect your life?

> *The world is so empty if one thinks only of mountains, rivers, and cities in it; but to know someone here and there who sympathizes with us, with whom we also in silent agreement, continue to live on, only this turns the earth into an inhabited garden for us.*
>
> — JOHANN WOLFGANG V. GOETHE

When did you learn to drive? Did you enjoy learning? Who taught you? If you don't drive, why not?

Everywhere, giant finned cars nose forward like fish.
— ROBERT LOWELL

Do you have any car stories? Bus, trolley, train, plane, bicycle, moped, horse?

Tell about your all-time favorite job or any others you want to record.

Back of the job—the dreamer who's making the dream come true!
— BERTON BRALEY

I like work; it fascinates. I can sit and look at it for hours. I love to keep it by me. The idea of getting rid of it merely breaks my heart.
— JEROME K. JEROME

Tell about your first job. How did you get it? What did you do? Who were the people involved and how did you relate to them? Were you aware of the politics and intrigues, if any?

It's all in the day's work, as the huntsman said when the lion ate him.
— CHARLES KINGSLEY

What were your bad habits? Do you still have them? Anything new? Who reminded you of them and how did they do it?

A man must have his faults.
— GAIUS PETRONIUS

60

Were you ever seriously ill or injured? How did it affect your life?

How sickness enlarges the dimensions of a man's self to himself.
— CHARLES LAMB

He's hardly ever sick at sea.
— W.S. GILBERT

What was your most outrageous daydream? What was your favorite spot for daydreaming?

This tale is a fragment from the life of dreams.
— S.T. COLERIDGE

Which of your dreams came true? Which are still pending? Which have you let go?

Do you want to write or draw your favorite fantasy?

63

What treasures have you lost? What was special about them?

There, little girl, don't cry.
— JAMES WHITCOMB RILEY

Tell about the treasures you have found or were given to you.

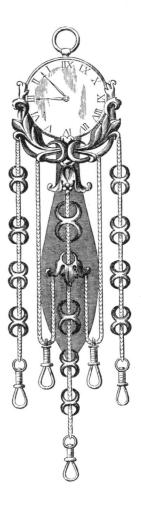

Are you, were you, in a committed relationship? Share some of your stories.

Have you had children? Write your favorite parent-child stories. If you haven't had a child, write a story about that.

What are the things you wish you could remember?

We were searching to rediscover the first seed so that the ancient drama could begin again.
— GEORGE SEFERIS

What are some things you wish you could forget?

Those who'll play with cats must expect to be scratched.
— MIGUEL DE CERVANTES

69

What things did you once believe that you no longer believe?

What are some things you don't WANT to believe?

Who's on first, What's on second, I Don't Know is on third.
— LOU COSTELLO AND BUD ABBOTT

What are some of the things you wish you had never found out?

When I make a mistake it's a beaut!
— FIORELLO H. LAGUARDIA
To travel hopefully is a better thing than to arrive.
— ROBERT LOUIS STEVENSON

What are some things you wish you had discovered sooner?

Four be the things I am wiser to know: idleness, sorrow, a friend, and a lover.
— DOROTHY PARKER

73

What are some things you still don't understand?

Is sex necessary?
— JAMES THURBER

74

Are you certain of anything?

> *It is better to know some of the questions than all of the answers.*
> — JAMES THURBER

What are some things you hope you never forget?

Just know your lines and don't bump into the furniture.
— SPENCER TRACY

What parts of your story do you hope others will remember and pass on?

Here lies my past. Goodbye I have kissed it;
Thank you, kids, I wouldn't have missed it.
— OGDEN NASH

Goodbye to All That
— ROBERT GRAVES

At last the secret is out, as it always must come in the end.
The delicious story is ripe to tell to the intimate friend.

78   — W.H. AUDEN